Abraham Lincoln

A biography of an American President

Table of Contents

Introduction

Thank you for taking the time to read this book on Abraham Lincoln.

This book covers the topic of Abraham Lincoln and will serve as a short biography of his life, achievements, tribulations, and legacy.

Throughout the following chapters, you will discover much about the life and impact of Abraham Lincoln. You will learn about his childhood, his time as a lawyer, his impact as a politician and President, as well as details of his untimely death.

At the completion of this book you will have a good understanding of Abraham Lincoln and the incredible legacy he has, as possibly the greatest US President in history!

Once again, thanks for choosing this book, I hope you find it to be both enjoyable and informative!

Chapter 1: Who Was Abraham Lincoln

Abraham Lincoln is one of the most historic leaders of the United States of America. He was the sixteenth President of the nation and was President during the American Civil War.

This was a time of turmoil when conflicting ideals clashed. He was not fortunate enough to be just a spectator in the tide of events that went on in his day. He was there at the forefront.

He was at the very helm and was openly struggling to gain control of the proverbial wheel that would sway which direction the fledgling country would go. The good news is that he was no stranger to hardships and it would seem that he was at home with adversity and trial.

His victory in the elections that landed him in the White House was a double-edged sword so to speak. On the one hand it was a moment for celebration since it was a time for new beginnings and a time for change. On the other hand, it caused a crisis for the entire country.

Democrats from the southern states felt that it was only a matter of time before the new President would make moves to abolish slavery. But slavery, freedom, and equality among men were not the only moral grounds or doctrines that were being shaken or put to the test.

Another question was whether the individual states held the higher authority or did the federal government. One of the grounds for the continuance of the practice of slavery was the fact that there were those who believed that the sovereignty of the states superseded all.

The Civil War began as a fight for the preservation of the Union. Literally millions of soldiers were conscripted on both the pro and anti-slavery sides of the conflict. Not everyone agreed with this course of action – this included some of the men and women in the north.

Abraham Lincoln assumed extralegal powers, and riots that broke out were quelled by the force of the Union's army. He even declared martial law – but this was not done so that he could personally gain. He exerted executive authority like no other President of the United States in order to preserve the unity of the nation.

The Civil War progressed from preserving the Union, to fighting for freedom in January of 1863 after the Emancipation Proclamation was made. The Gettysburg Address was a hallmark piece of oration and it was the keynote that marked the ending of an era – an era of slavery and injustice.

Lincoln was in deep water both in his public as well as in his private affairs. On the one hand he had a nation to hold together and a people he had to fight for. On the other there was the matter of his own personal losses.

His son died during the time of national turmoil. His own state of mind was one thing and the onset of depression on his wife was another burden that he had to bear. Lincoln himself fell into deep despair yet was able to claw his way back from personal tragedies and again return to national leadership.

The majority of historians consider him as the greatest American President in the nation's history. This is thanks to the way he handled the executive seat during the Civil War. This exemplary role had a tremendous impact on the moral and political character of the United States.

Chapter 2: Before He Became President

Everyone hails Abraham Lincoln as the man who issued the Emancipation Proclamation and the President who preserved the Union. But who was he before he became this highly regarded man in history?

Abraham Lincoln was born on February 12, 1809. He wasn't born into a prestigious family. His first home was a log cabin in modest surroundings in Hardin County, Kentucky. He didn't have a nice paved floor when he was young – the family living space consisted of a dirt floor.

Conflict with His Father

Abe Lincoln's father was called Thomas – a man who could not read and one who could hardly spell his own name. Needless to say, Abraham didn't like his father that much. They were two diametrically opposed individuals and they often argued.

Thomas Lincoln himself was born poor. He is often described as a stern man by historians and those who chronicled Abraham Lincoln's life. Thomas raised his family in rural Kentucky. However, in search for better opportunities in life, he decided to move his entire family to Indiana's frontier.

Thomas Lincoln's profession was carpentry and farming. He moved the family into frontier territory when Abe was only 7 years of age. Out there he built a log cabin, which was nowhere near elegant, but was functional.

It was 360 square feet, and it kept the cold out as well as it could. That became home for little Abraham, his mother, and his older sister Sarah. All went well for a time, but little Abraham bonded more with his mother than his father.

Death of His Mother

Two years after their move to Indiana, Abe's mother died after ingesting poisoned milk. After a short time later, his father remarried. Some children never got along with their stepmothers, but Abraham bonded with Sarah Bush Johnston, his father's second wife.

In fact, when arguments arose between Abe and his father, Sarah often took Abe's side in the argument. Note that this happened frequently. That is probably one of the reasons why the young Abraham never really liked his father.

For her part, Sarah was a truly bright woman. Other than the emotional support she gave to Abe, she also encouraged him to get an education. However, there was very little chance of that occurring in the tough rural areas of Indiana.

American frontier life was difficult for everyone back in the early 1800s. There was almost always no time for school, which is why Abe only had limited formal education. Struggling against poverty, the family had to do everything from farm chores to uprooting tree stumps to get by.

The young Abraham retreated from the hard life to books which he read by the fireplace. This habit of reading books became his comfort and strength, and it would eventually serve him well in life.

Abe was later described as a self-taught man who gained knowledge on his own.

Entrepreneurial Spirit

Abe Lincoln was definitely an entrepreneur. He had a number of business ventures in his lifetime. And just like any entrepreneur, he lost in some and he also won in some. Signs of his entrepreneurial spirit could be witnessed when he was just 17 years old.

He loved river boat riding and he even found work as a hand on a ferryboat. He eventually built his own flatboat two years after his employ. He ferried farm produce along the Mississippi River all the way to New Orleans.

When he got to New Orleans, he sold his flatboat and then walked all the way home. Now, even though he and his father weren't really on good terms he dutifully gave all of his earnings to his father. He resented doing that, but he felt that he had to because it was expected of him. This of course gives us a hint into his character.

The Move to Illinois

Thomas Lincoln moved his family again. By this time Abraham had turned 21. They moved west of Decatur in Illinois. Abraham helped his father build their log home, which was about the same size as the one they previously had.

Later on, once the family was settled, Abe once more built himself another flatboat to ferry farm produce. This time he was an independent contractor and he made his run downriver. But things were different this time. After moving the produce, he never returned home. By 1821 Abraham Lincoln lived on his own, settling in New Salem.

Life in New Salem

In New Salem, Abraham made a reputation for himself by being the bookish, good-natured young man. He became quite a popular figure in town and he endeared himself to the townsfolk. His wit and intellect brought about by his frequent reading marked him as someone different from the other boys.

Other than being an intellectual sort of person, Abe also stood out physically. Standing at a full 6 foot 4 inches, you could easily spot him in any crowd. He was tall, he was lanky, and his nose was most likely in a book. No wonder he stood out.

However, do not mistake him for a nerd. Remember that his childhood was filled with hard labor and Abe was no stranger to tedious work with his hands. He was physically strong – a true man of the frontier.

On one occasion, the town bully made the mistake of trying to have his way with Abe. He ended up getting out wrestled and humiliated. This of course amazed and won the adoration of Abraham's neighbors.

The General Store

Abraham worked in a general store while he was in New Salem. During the early 1800s the general store was a social place where you could meet anyone and everyone in town.

This was where the town's people usually congregated to discuss everything from the weather to politics. It was the town's informal meeting place, and there Abraham Lincoln got to know the local community very well.

In the midst of the crowd he found his latent ability to amaze his audience using his wit, charm, and integrity. A lot of the people in New Salem were illiterate, and that made Lincoln's ability to read really valuable. He would delight them with what he learned from the pages of the books and publications of the day.

And so, it was six months after his arrival at New Salem, that his ambition took the driver's seat. He publicly announced that he was running for a seat at the state's legislature. He filed his candidacy as an independent.

Unfortunately, a few weeks later after filing his candidacy came the outbreak of the Black Hawk War. Abe seemed to put his young political ambitions aside and volunteered to fight in the war.

The Black Hawk War

Was Abraham Lincoln a charismatic person? There is no doubt that he truly was. Even when he was a young man during the Black Hawk War he was selected by his peers in the company as their temporary captain.

After his appointment as captain, the company marched off to war under his leadership. They marched for 30 days looking for the enemy, but they found no one. What eventually happened was a military stint that saw no action.

We can deduce from the record that perhaps this lack of military action frustrated Abraham at this time. You see, since this first campaign was all but eventful, he again signed up for another "tour" as we call it today.

During his second war stint he served as a private. This time he wasn't in the militia or regular army. He was part of the Independent Spy Corps. Their mission was to track down Chief Black Hawk and scour the entire Wisconsin area. This stint also proved to be futile since Lincoln also didn't see any action during his service with the Spy Corps.

Chapter 3: Early Political Career

After the Black Hawk War, Abraham Lincoln returned to New Salem to resume his election campaign. Unfortunately, his duty in the war prevented him from doing any campaign work. That means he didn't have enough time on his hands to make a mark in the political arena.

However, he was the winning candidate in his town of New Salem. There were a total of 300 votes and Lincoln won 277 of them. That was a landslide victory – at least in his town.

The results though weren't the same in the rest of the territories. Remember that his was a very large district at the time. It definitely would take time and considerable effort to make himself known to everyone. There was a total of 13 aspirants at the time, and Lincoln landed only the 8th spot after all the votes were cast.

The Path of a Rebound

Lincoln didn't let this defeat bring him down. He retreated to where he was most at home – with his books. He was determined to get his act together, and so focused his energies to the study of law.

And so, he read law books and educated himself on the subject.

Lincoln Law Cases

He later took the bar and was able to obtain his law license in 1837. He then represented different people in various cases. His law practice involved both criminal and civil cases. The cases involved included such issues as debt collection, bootlegging, assault, breach of contract, and other issues.

For example, in 1853 Lincoln represented Higgins in *People ex rel. Stevenson v Higgins, 15 Ill 110.* This was concerning the removal from a hospital by the board of trustees.

Another trial was on 1857, Sprague v. Illinois River Railroad Co. 19 Ill 174. This was regarding an amendment to the charter of the railroad company regarding the liability of its stock holders.

The following is a list of some of the other cases that involved the representation by Abraham Lincoln as a lawyer:

- Wolfe vs. Snyder, 9 Ds., 1851-1853
- Taylor v. Wright, A.D.S., 1843
- Ten Brook, Adm. vs. Guthrie, 8 Ds., 1851-1852
- Speed vs. Reeves, D. 3 p., 1853
- Snyder vs. Wolfe papers, A.D.S., 1851
- Sommerville vs. Bailey, 18 Ds., 1853
- Rucker vs. Early, D., 1840
- Shelby v. Shelby, A.D.S., [ca. 1840]
- Reed vs. Henderson, 17 Ds., 1852
- Rives vs. Martin and Booth, 31 Ds., 1852-1853
- Nolan vs. Hunter, 16 Ds., 1841
- Paddock vs. Snyder, 2 Ds., 1851-1853
- Merrow et al. vs. Ambo et al., A.D.S., 1859
- Neale vs. Britton, A.D.S., 1850
- Matkin vs. Brown, A.D.S., 1850
- Mayo vs. Benson, D., 1851
- Lilley vs. Lilley, 4 Ds, 1855
- McCutchen vs. Allen complaint, A.D.S., 1842

Note that this is only a partial list. Abraham Lincoln did not win every case – he wasn't superhuman. He however learned a lot of lessons from his dealings with the courts.

Now, going back to his days in New Salem, the new lawyer took on whatever case he could. On top of this, he also participated in the functions of the Whig party. He even functioned as the secretary those meetings.

In spite of the political party that he belonged to at the time, Andrew Jackson, the President of the democrats saw potential in the bright young man. And so, he appointed Lincoln to be New Salem's postmaster.

It should be noted that at this time Lincoln did not support Jackson. He voiced his support for Henry Clay in 1832, yet Andrew Jackson appointed him anyway.

As postmaster he only earned $55 annually, which is by all measures truly meager. But Abe wasn't one to complain .

He was rather proactive despite his lot in life. Court cases were hard to come by, but he did what he could and represented clients when they came. However, to further supplement his meager income, he also handled some of the town's routine legal work which was often only charged with modest fees.

At the time Abe also worked as a county deputy surveyor. He also did a lot of manual labor like splitting rails and chopping wood. He was a hard worker. His upbringing on the frontier helped to mold him into a man of industry who avoided idling his time away.

Initial Political Success

He ran once more for a seat at the legislature during the election of 1834 – the big difference is that this second time he was in the winner's circle. His second run was interesting since even the democrats voted for him. Was this perhaps due to the fact that he avoided non-partisan posturing? Perhaps it was.

His strategy for this election was completely different though, and it worked. This time he gave only a few speeches, he made no promises, and he didn't declare any platform statement.

Okay so, what did he do then? In short, he socialized with everyone in the county. He made it a point to visit every family. He shook hands with everyone – Whig or Democrat it didn't matter. He told them jokes and endeared himself to pretty much everybody – even political rivals.

What makes this strategy interesting is the fact that he won again in his succeeding campaigns from 1836 to 1840. However, every time he got reelected his political leanings became more obvious. For instance, he was in favor of chartering a state bank and he supported all the possible internal improvements that were put forward.

He did have political leanings just like everybody else. For instance, while in office the young legislator usually voted for Whig candidates.

One of his political moves seemed to foreshadow his true path in politics. In 1837, Abraham Lincoln was one of the five legislators who opposed a resolution that was intended to condemn abolitionists. It was 5 of them versus 78 other legislators.

Another thing that made him stand out was his response to the killing of Elijah Parish Lovejoy in 1838. Lovejoy was a newspaper editor and an abolitionist. He was killed in Alton, Illinois while defending his printing presses from an attack by a mob. The mob was composed of pro-slavery citizens.

Lincoln gave a speech in the Springfield Young Men's Lyceum. In that speech he highlighted the dangers of citizens resorting to violence instead of reason. He told the audience how dangerous it was to democracy when people do not let votes and the rules of law prevail.

His political path was made more definite come 1840 when he denounced Martin Van Buren, the Democratic candidate. He instead supported William Henry Harrison, the populist war hero who was of course, a Whig candidate.

His reason for denouncing Van Buren was due to the fact that the man voted in favor of giving free blacks the right to vote. In his speeches, Lincoln appealed to the racism that was prevalent in the citizens of Illinois at the time. Of course, Lincoln opposed slavery. However, just like his peers at the time, he was only in favor of giving a limited form of liberty to blacks which meant he was not in favor of giving them citizenship rights.

Chapter 4: Political Maneuvering and Political Issues

In the following years in his career as a politician, Abraham Lincoln became more vocal with regard to different political issues. He eventually also learned to use a variety of political maneuvers, which made him a better political leader and eventually a better President. His experience over the years helped prepare him for a lot of rough and tangle with politicians who opposed him and his views.

The Mexican-American War

Abraham Lincoln served four terms in the Illinois state legislature until 1841. After four terms, Lincoln left office and returned to his private law practice. However, the public life called for him again five years after. In 1846 he accepted the Whig nomination for a seat in the US House of Representatives. He was to represent the seventh congressional district of Illinois.

Unfortunately, 10 days after his nomination, the Mexican-American war broke out. Lincoln again wisely put his previous election strategy to use – don't say anything about the current crisis. And guess what. It worked.

He actually won the district by a huge majority. However, he only revealed his real position on the war when he gave a speech on the Congressional Floor.

In that scathing speech he criticized James Polk, the current President of the country, and challenged the man's position on the current conflict with Mexico. Polk asserted that it was the Mexicans that started the war when they attacked their troops on US soil.

Lincoln stated that the President had misrepresented the situation. The territory where the US troops were attacked was on a contested area by both countries. This speech and its key points shocked everyone. It was nothing less than a blatant attack from a congressman that essentially unknown nationally. What made matters worse was the fact that the State of Illinois was solidly in support of the war with Mexico.

It was a bold position and it gave a solid shock even to Lincoln's friends. However, they weren't the views of only one man. Every other Whig congressman actually held the same view, but it was only Lincoln who had the courage to voice out what was on everyone's minds.

This was actually part of his strategy in the world of politics. Lincoln was rapidly learning the tricks of the trade at this point in time.

Remaining Politically Significant

He also wanted his name to remain in the public's collective mind long after the election period. So, in 1848 he campaigned for Zachary Taylor, the Whig presidential candidate. He gave his campaign speech in Maryland and Massachusetts in front of a national audience.

That helped cement his position as a possible candidate in coming elections. He then retired temporarily from any political activities, before settling in Springfield. He returned to his law practice from 1849 to 1854. This time, his law practice was more successful than ever. His clientele was more diverse, and his work also included handling railroad interests.

In 1854, he again won a seat at the state legislature, but he resigned immediately when the senatorial elections came around. He lost in his bid at the 9th ballot. You see, in those days the election of senators was done by the state legislators.

At this time the Whig Party had officially become defunct, and so Abraham Lincoln moved to the Republican Party in 1856. Many of the former Whigs who opposed slavery moved into this newly formed national party. It should be noted that the Republicans were firmly against slavery.

The new political party was determined to get the Kansas-Nebraska Act repealed. Doing that would prevent the extension of the practice of slavery into the western states. They were also pushing for the immediate admission of Kansas into the Union.

Another issue that they were pressing for was the repeal of the Ostend Manifesto. This manifesto was calling for the annexation of Cuba. Why were they against this? Well, you should know that back then slavery was legal in Cuba.

His position in politics made Lincoln a top candidate in Illinois. He got the nomination for Vice President, but he didn't win in the Republican convention in Philadelphia.

The Lincoln-Douglas Debates of 1858

In spite of their best efforts, the Republicans lost their bid for the US Presidency, and James Buchanan of the Democratic Party was elected President of the country. Two years later Abraham Lincoln was able to secure the Republican nomination to the country's senate.

This placed him in way of Stephen A. Douglas, who was running for his reelection – it was going to be his third term. Lincoln and Douglas had been rivals before; during their days in the Illinois state capital.

Seven debates between these two fine candidates were scheduled all over the state of Illinois. The entire soiree totaled about 70 days-worth of engagements. Some factors lent to the popularity of these debates.

They include the following:

- Stephen Douglas was the Democratic Party's best speaker at the stump
- Douglas was regarded as the "Little Giant" of his party

- Douglas was also one of the key people behind the 1850 Compromise.
- The debate on the slavery issue was the hottest topic in the country
- The issues that the two were going to argue over have already divided the nation sharply. Some of the encounters over the said issues turned out to be quite violent.

This was the biggest debate in the history of the nation at the time. Journalists from every outfit accompanied the parties to the debates, and they offered their commentary.

Chapter 5: The Lincoln-Douglas Debates

The series of 7 debates between Abraham Lincoln and Stephen Douglas has been highly regarded by historians and political scientists. This was during the Illinois state election campaign in 1858. People have viewed it as one of the most, if not the most, significant moments in the history of US politics.

The issues that they discussed at length during these debates were of critical importance. At its core, they touched on the sectional conflict that all the states had over the slavery issue, as well as the rights of each state to enact and enforce their own laws.

We can say that the arguments that both men presented during these debates represent some of the most influential political discourse in history. Lincoln himself even remarked that the issues that he and Douglas discussed will long remain a topic of rational discourse long after "these poor tongues of Judge Douglas and myself shall be silent." Indeed, the subjects that they covered and argued are nothing less than classic since they touch political, ethical, philosophical, and moral tenets the world over.

Important Points to Consider

There are of course aspects of these debates that get overlooked. For instance, we should bear in mind that these debates were rather part of a larger campaign. These debates, as well as other political debates elsewhere, serve to obtain certain political objectives. Most of all, getting into the context of these discussions, they reflect the point of view, rhetoric, and of course the character of the people in the mid-19th century.

Political Motivations

Douglas was one of the leaders of the Democratic Party. He has been a congressman since 1843. On top of that he was a prominent national spokesman for the Democrats. He was regarded as the "Little Giant" of their party. He was seeking a reelection for the third time in the United States Senate.

Lincoln on the other hand was campaigning for Douglas' seat at the senate, and he was from the Republican Party. Lincoln was mostly an unknown as far as the national public was concerned. That means the popularity of these debates was in part due to the stature of Stephen A. Douglas.

The issues discussed included sectional as well as slavery issues. Many theorized that the outcome of these debates would determine if the Union was still viable or not.

One Washington paper announced in its headlines "The battle of the Union is to be fought in Illinois."

***Historical Notes:** So, why did they schedule 7 debates? This was due to the fact that there are seven Congressional districts in Illinois. As stated elsewhere, senators were elected not by popular vote back then, but by state legislatures. It was only in 1913 when this practice was discontinued.*

In spite of that fact, Lincoln and Douglas made their debates public and they appealed to the people directly. The increased significance of this debate was fueled by several factors including the instability of the current party system, the volatility of the slavery issue, and the sectional animosity that was involved.

The Issue on Kansas Statehood

During these debates, Stephen Douglas was in a slightly precarious position. He opposed the admission of Kansas as a slave state. By doing so he went against current US President James Buchanan, and of course the leadership of his party.

Douglas didn't want to let the State of Kansas be admitted under the grounds of the Lecompton constitution, which was of course pro-slavery. It has been widely believed that the Lecompton constitution was enacted via voter fraud. Douglas and others believed that "border ruffians" from Missouri manipulated the votes.

That is why Douglas stressed that the said constitution is unrepresentative of the state's actual majority opinion. He also appealed to the Northern Democrats as well as the Republicans in his efforts. He also took on the largely popular sovereignty stance on this issue.

When he did that, Douglas was then accused of party treason by the Southern Democrats. Note that the Republicans supported Douglas in Congress regarding this issue. With that said, it is interesting to note that Buchanan along with his allies supported Lincoln's candidacy simply because of their animosity towards Douglas. This was of course a strange and curious alignment in the history of American politics.

Lincoln's Task

From the start, Lincoln understood what he had to do during these debates. First off, he knew that he needed to take the moral high ground, which would stop some Republicans from voting for Douglas – the idea was to divide the Democrats.

With that end in mind he began his campaign a bit early, in June 16, 1858 in Springfield, Illinois, with one of the grandest pieces of rhetoric in the history of the United States, which is called the House Divided speech.

This talk was regarded by many as one of the most important speeches ever made. It held a powerful message regarding the moral crisis of slavery. In his talk he pointed out that the moral crisis of slavery will never be truly over until the United States as one nation became completely slave free.

In this speech he quoted from the Bible the very words of Christ himself, appealing to the Christian foundations of his listeners, "A house divided against itself cannot stand."

He then moved the people's attention towards Stephen Douglas and the currently popular sovereignty perspective. He then pointed out multiple episodes where settlers in the territories would fight over the issue of slavery just to get the upper hand.

Douglas's Counter

Lincoln further charged Douglas as being part of a master plan to extend the practice of slavery to all states within the Union. He also made a strong emphasis on his view that slavery was immoral.

He further stressed that the practice of slavery is a violation of the Declaration of Independence and its most fundamental principles; i.e. that all men are created equal. He also stated in his talk that allowing the practice to continue in the country is contrary to what the founding fathers envisioned.

Finally, Lincoln pointed out that it is ultimately the duty of the federal government to extinguish the practice of slavery and resolve the conflict for everybody.

Further, he also stated that it should be prevented from expanding westward. The bottom line of his reasoning was that slavery is wrong. And with the stance that Douglas had chosen; i.e. being indifferent to the issue, simply meant that he was being passive to something that is absolutely and morally wrong.

So how did Stephen Douglas counter these assertions?

Since Abraham Lincoln spoke with ad hominem in his arguments, Douglas countered with ad hominem of his own. He countered his opponent's assertions by first portraying Lincoln as one of the radical abolitionists.

He disagreed with Lincoln's point that the founding fathers of the land were against the practice of slavery. He pointed out that many of the men who signed the Declaration of Independence were in fact slave owners. He stressed that even Thomas Jefferson and George Washington owned slaves even after they helped create the great nation of the United States.

He further accused Abraham Lincoln of being a dangerous fanatic and also an abolitionist at heart. He said that Lincoln's policies would lead to nothing more than racial equality and racial consolidation. The tactic was simple – all he needed to do was to appeal to the racial prejudice of his hearers – the voters of Illinois.

He did not meet Lincoln's moral high ground position head on. Rather, he played down whatever moral issue that his opponent had raised.

He stressed that the power to decide whether a state would practice slavery should be left with the local community. With regard to the accusation that he was pushing slavery to spread out to the west, he pointed out that this would not occur simply because of economic reasons. He said that there would be no economic cause or reason for western states to adopt the practice, thus any possible spread westward was improbable.

And then there was also the issue of the Dred Scott decision that was made by the Supreme Court. In that decision, the court favored and defended the property rights of slave owners. In spite of that decision, Douglas still asserted his points in his Freeport Doctrine – his speech countering Lincoln's that was delivered in Freeport, Illinois, which stressed that the people themselves could decide to keep the practice of slavery outside of their own territories.

Furthermore, Douglas also pointed out that local communities can decide not to have police laws so as not to protect slave owners and prevent the institution of slavery on the local level.

He also warned his listeners that the people should never judge political issues using moral grounds. He pointed out that doing so would make the people's emotions spill over and it may lead to civil war.

Finally, Douglas summarized by saying that the issue at hand was simple. It simply falls on how people view a confederacy, which means that it is all about two conflicting ideologies. Should we see the confederacy as a nation of equal and sovereign states, or is it a federalist empire of consolidated states?

The Issue of Limited Racial Equality

The issue of racial equality was the last topic that Lincoln and Douglas debated on. This issue in particular was the issue that Lincoln had difficulty answering, which would seem surprising to some considering the fact that he was regarded as the great emancipator. Again, it would help if we put everything in its proper context.

You see Lincoln couldn't simply declare that the Declaration of Independence gives African Americans the same God given rights as White Americans. That would leave him vulnerable to the race baiting that Douglas has expertly used during these debates.

Douglas even challenged Lincoln by saying that either African Americans were absolute equals to white Americans or they were not. And that was a pretty bold assertion to make, and one that appealed greatly to the audience at the time of these debates.

Lincoln on the other hand contended that there were social as well as physical differences between the races. These differences are the things that would prevent both races from living together in perfect equality.

However, having said that, it did not mean that the African Americans could never be truly free. For example, in his Free Labor doctrine, which is a Republican ideology by the way, Lincoln pointed out that African Americans should be entitled to the natural rights as they are enumerated in the Declaration of Independence. These rights include the "right to life, liberty, and the pursuit of happiness."

An interesting and all too powerful footnote to all of this is that Lincoln, just like other Republicans of his time, believed in a limited racial equality. He opposed the idea of giving African Americans the right to vote.

He also believed that they should not intermarry with other races. They were not to be given the right to hold public office. And Lincoln also believed that African Americans shouldn't be given the right to sit in juries. Nevertheless, he believed that African Americans had the equal right to earn their just rewards for the labors that they perform.

Aftermath

After the series of seven debates were over, the republicans had a slight lead when it came to the popular votes. However, it should be remembered that senators were elected by the state legislatures, and not by popular vote.

There was a malapportionment of legislative districts which ran in favor of the Democrats. And so, Douglas won the elections over Lincoln with 54 votes to 46.

However, the debates elevated Lincoln to a higher status within the Republican Party and eventually, they made him their leader. It also earned him a national reputation, thus making him a strong candidate for the Presidency.

Chapter 6: Winning the White House and The Advent Civil War

On the day of the elections in 1859, voters turned in their ballots to elect members of the state legislature. In turn, the state legislators reelected Stephen Douglas as a senator, gaining the victory for his 3rd term.

It was not a total loss for Lincoln and the Republicans. In fact, they gained the majority of the popular votes. This was a signal that there was a shift in the political character in the state of Illinois.

On top of that, Lincoln obtained notable popularity in the north. He was later invited to campaign for other Republican candidates, and his name frequently came up when discussing candidates for the Presidency.

Stephen A. Douglas on the other hand further alienated the Democratic Party's leadership, particularly the party's leader at the time, then President James Buchanan. Douglas was later stripped of his power in the senate. This bit of ruckus contributed to the schism within the Democratic Party.

For his part, Lincoln bolstered his profile in 1860. That year he delivered another speech at New York City's Cooper Union that moved his audience and captured the hearts of the voting public. In May of that year, the republicans selected Lincoln as their official candidate for the Presidency.

There were other candidates of course like New York's Senator William H. Seward, and other powerful contenders. This was an interesting turn of events considering the fact that Lincoln only had one congressional term under his proverbial belt.

The Road to the White House

Douglas and Lincoln once again faced off in the Presidential elections. Lincoln represented the Republicans and Douglas was the candidate for the northern Democrats. The Democratic Party at this time was a "house divided." Note that Kentucky's John C. Breckenridge was chosen by the southern Democrats.

Another party to the elections in that year was John Bell who was the face of the newly formed Constitutional Union Party. This time, the environment of the electoral contest was different.

The vote in the South was split between Breckenridge and Bell. Lincoln on the other hand won the majority of the North which then carried the Electoral College. And thus, with their houses divided, Lincoln won the White House.

Advent of Civil War

There were several years of sectional tension, even before a northerner who was particularly anti-slavery came along to become the 16th President of the United States. It was not like Abraham Lincoln brought about the Civil War entirely by himself.

However, when Lincoln was elected President, that was enough to drive the pro-slavery south over the brink. When Lincoln was sworn in to the White House in March of 1861, seven of the pro slavery states in the south seceded from the Union. They then formed the Confederate States of America.

Philosophical Differences

Why did the south secede from the Union? It was in part a matter of philosophy, actually. The way the southern states saw it, the United States was to them a compact of Southern states. In their point of view, the states that joined into this compact had agreed to allow a national government to act as their agent. This meant the states that were part of this union of states never gave up their individual sovereignty.

It was their position from the beginning that any state could withdraw from the Union. In contrast, the northern states saw the Union as a more permanent bond. They saw it as a more perfect union. However, things may not exactly be what they thought if you consider the statements in the Articles of Confederation.

Of course, when you asked Abe Lincoln, he denied that the states ever had individual sovereignty. He further stated that the states had already accepted without any condition when they ratified the Constitution.

And then there was the point about the right to revolution – just as what the founding fathers did in their revolt against England. Abe Lincoln responded to this by stating that the right to revolt is more of a moral right, given the suppression of liberties and freedoms. And that is how it should be justified.

He further asked if the south could enumerate any liberties, freedoms, and rights that were trampled upon during his election as President? They of course couldn't find any since they were still afforded all the rights, liberties, and freedoms at the time when Lincoln was sworn into office.

Therefore, Lincoln concluded that there is no cause for standing by their right to revolution. What the southern states did when they seceded from the Union, according to Lincoln himself, was merely a "wicked exercise of physical power." The majority of northerners agreed with that line of reasoning. To them secession from the Union was nothing more than an act of treason which was definitely unconstitutional by all accounts.

A Reconciliatory Response

Lincoln did what had seemed to become a standard operating procedure for him – he kept quiet about the issue in public.

However, he sent private messages to key military officials and to members of congress.

In these messages he reiterated the promises he made during his campaign for President. This included not limiting or impairing the right of any state to slavery where it already existed.

To demonstrate his intent to keep his campaign promises in good faith, he even supported a thirteenth amendment to the constitution. This amendment was already passed by Congress and it would guarantee the practice of slavery in every state where it already existed.

Of course, Lincoln knew when and where to draw the line. For instance, when the Crittenden Compromise was put forward by Senator John J. Crittenden of Kentucky, he had to put his foot down on that matter.

The Crittenden Compromise called for several constitutional amendments as well as other guarantees for the slave states and slave owners. It would have impeded the powers of Congress to stop any interstate slave trade. The rest of the concessions it contained would undermine all the principles that Republicans stood for.

Civil War Begins

"In your hands, my dissatisfied fellow-countrymen, and not mine, is the momentous issue of civil war," Lincoln said in his inaugural speech. The following day he received a dispatch informing him that he must either abandon Fort Sumter or resupply it – the problem was that it was in confederate territory.

It can be attributed to Lincoln's genius in forcing the enemy to draw first blood. Lincoln sent unarmed supply ships to Fort Sumter. He also gave an advance notice of the peaceful intentions of the ships to confederate officials.

It was said that the new Confederate President, Jefferson Davis, did not blink. He ordered his general to compel the armed forces in Fort Sumter to surrender. It was in the morning of April 12, 1861 when the first shots were fired by confederate guns that forced Major Anderson to surrender the fort – and thus, Civil War had begun.

Chapter 7: Civil War

The American Civil War is in itself deserving of its own book for a more detailed discussion. Here, we will attempt to recount events that directly related to Abraham Lincoln.

Lincoln had to address a slew of interrelated issues with the coming war, which included the following:

- Finding the right generals
- Raising a volunteer army
- Marshaling the country's economy to support the war effort
- Dealing with the coming dissentions from home and at the battle front
- Preventing foreign countries from recognizing the confederacy as a legitimate government
- Conducting a war that would result in lasting peace
- Dealing with the issue of slavery in a world where most of the white men were anti-black

These challenges were definitely constant, and at times it was like plugging one hole only to find another had taken its place.

Radical Changes

Lincoln dismissed and appointed Officers and Generals in the army faster than you could blink. He even dismissed generals like George B. McClellan who won victories over Confederate forces led by General Robert E. Lee.

These dismissals came as a shock, but what Lincoln wanted was a General that would pursue every last confederate on the battlefield and end the fight effectively to the last man. He believed that if McClellan and others only did as he asked then the Civil War would have ended sooner.

The war continued for four and a half years, with more than 600,000 dead.

It took some time to find able Generals who would not allow confederates to escape intact to fight another day. He finally found the General that he wanted in Ulysses S. Grant, and his protégé General William Sherman. They pursued the enemy to the last man and they held their ground, never surrendering.

It took 2 full years before Lincoln could find Generals that served his purposes well. He retired a number of Generals, including McClellan, John Pope, Joseph Hooker, Ambrose E. Burnside, and George Gordon Meade. He was disappointed in them and replaced them as fast as he could.

Abe Lincoln also took an active part in the war. He visited soldier camps and he granted Presidential pardons to deserters as well as other soldiers who were to be executed for various crimes while serving in the army.

As the body count increased and the war raged on, the number of volunteers decreased. Lincoln turned to conscription to supplant the need for soldiers.

He had to marshal the country's economy and to do that he appointed efficient cabinet members who did their job well. Whenever a corrupt member of the cabinet was found, he was replaced immediately. He was good at finding men who were good at restoring honesty and efficiency to the department they presided over.

Emancipation

Lincoln enacted a gradual emancipation program. As expected, thousands of slaves fled from the south and joined the Union lines. Free African Americans from the north urged the President to act quickly.

He issued a preliminary emancipation proclamation on September 22, 1862 and finally his full Emancipation

Proclamation on January 1, 1863. This demonstrated the President's war powers. It should be noted that this famous decree only applied to territories that were not within confederate control. With that proclamation, the Lincoln administration made freedom and reunion become the main war effort.

Homestead Act

On May 20, 1862 Abraham Lincoln signed the Homestead Act into law. This law granted public lands to small farmers. This act stated that any family man could obtain a total of 160 acres of public land by paying a small registration fee and living on the said land for five years. As per this act, one could own the said land by paying just $1.25 per acre.

By the end of the Civil War, a total of 15,000 homestead claims had been filed. Many more claims followed after the war.

During the war, Abraham Lincoln suspended certain civil liberties. For instance, he suspended the right to habeas corpus and he was criticized for doing so. He also declared martial law in certain areas as well. Lincoln explained that such measures were necessary in order to win the war.

A final note for the war was his very own and very popular Gettysburg Address. It was a short speech – only about 272 words, and it was for the dedication of the new national cemetery. In it, he harked back to the founding fathers, human equality, and human equality. This is actually one of the most often quoted speeches in history.

Chapter 8: The Assassination of the President

Hours after the Confederate President Jefferson Davis fled from Richmond, Virginia, the capital of the Confederacy, Abraham Lincoln walked its streets on April 3, 1865 to the cheers of thousands of African Americans.

A few miles from that location, General Robert E. Lee of the Confederate Army made the toughest decision of his life—surrendering to General Grant. He was facing the inevitable. He had 35,000 men who were all weary of war. Grant on the other hand had 120,000 bluecoats of the Union army.

The actual and formal surrender occurred on April 9. As a respect for the valor of the Confederate soldiers, their officers were allowed to retain their swords.

Five days later, the victorious President Lincoln was in Ford's Theater in Washington DC. He was watching Laura Keene's 'Our American Cousin', a light comedy. His bodyguard was not at his post, strangely enough, when a dark clad figure burst into their private box and shot Abraham Lincoln in the back of his head, at point blank range.

Mary Todd Lincoln tried to shield her husband but wasn't successful. The assassin, leapt from the balcony and landed on the stage, where he shouted "Sic semper Tyrannis!"

Ten days later, the assassin, John Wilkes Booth was found hiding in a barn. They set fire to the barn but couldn't clearly tell if Booth was shot dead during the standoff, burned in the fire, or if he shot himself.

The wound to the back of his head claimed Abe Lincoln's life the following day in the early morning. This death muted any celebration that was to be had after winning the war against the confederacy. They marched his body along a 1,700-mile route through small villages and towns.

Chapter 9: Fun Facts About Honest Abe

There are many fun facts about Abraham Lincoln, and this chapter details some of the best! Note that the trivia that we have collected below isn't arranged in any particular order. And now, for the fun facts:

1. Don't call him Abe – he doesn't like it. In fact, he hated it. Don't call him Honest Abe either. Apparently, he was the type of guy who preferred to be called by his last name.

2. The day when he was assassinated at Ford's Theater he actually had a guest by the name of Ulysses S. Grant with him. Grant cancelled his attendance at the last second. You can guess that if he was there then both of them may have gotten shot.

3. Who was Lincoln's tailor? It was none other than the Brooks Brothers.

4. Exactly one year after he died, Fido, his dog, was also "assassinated" by a drunken guy.

5. What's up with Abe's hat? It's an iconic symbol, right? Well, it did have another use other than being a fashion signature – he actually kept important documents in that hat.

6. Dueling was common practice during Lincoln's time, and in the name of defending his honor, Abraham Lincoln was scheduled to duel one time. Fortunately, it got cancelled at the last minute.

7. Believe it or not Abraham Lincoln didn't have a middle name. He was born, got registered as a voter, practiced law, and became President with just those two names – Abraham and Lincoln.

8. Just like many folks of his time, he did not belong to an organized church. And just like many other folks in those

frontier days, he also read the Bible regularly, but just didn't feel like joining any kind of organized religion.

9. His very first bid in a Presidential ticket was an utter failure. He was an unknown back then in 1856 and he lost in his first try at the Republican Convention.

10. Believe it or not, Abraham Lincoln was actually a wrestler. Wrestling was one of the pastimes in those days and good old Abe was pretty good at it given his size and skill. Abe had an awesome wrestling record – he only lost once out of all 300 of his wrestling matches.

11. Honest Abe was a true animal lover. He never went fishing or hunting during his lifetime.

12. Clean living wasn't a thing back then – that meant all the boys smoked or chewed tobacco; but not Abraham Lincoln. He never smoked, and he never chewed tobacco. He even preferred not to drink while doing his job at the White House. He was for the most part a simple man with simple tastes.

13. Lincoln was a suffragette even before he became President of the United States. That means he wanted to give women the right to vote – an idea that seemed foreign to many at the time.

14. We mentioned that Lincoln at one point in his life practiced law and we do have court records of him performing in that office. The amazing part of this is, he did the job without any formal schooling!

15. Of all the Presidents of this country he was the only one to ever own a patent. Lincoln actually invented a device that could free any steam boat that had run aground.

16. He was utterly obsessed with cats and he had lots of cats in the White House.

17. From his pictures, paintings, and even in the statues that memorialized him, you will rarely see an Abraham Lincoln smile. There may be a deep-seated reason for his overall demeanor – he battled with depression for much of his life.

18. One of his wrestling opponents (his most popular opponent at that) had a son who was accused of murder. Lincoln defended that man in court on murder charges.

19. Other than being a lawyer, Lincoln also became an Illinois circuit court judge.

20. Guess who was the first United States President to ever be assassinated? It was good old Abe.

21. There were other attempts on his life before his assassination. In one attempt back in 1864, his stovepipe hat ended up with a bullet hole in it – but luckily, Abe was uninjured.

22. The White House used to have a stable back in those days and that was where Lincoln kept his animals. Sadly, these creatures that he protected and cared for died in a stable fire.

23. People conducted séances when Lincoln's son died, and guess what – he took part in them.

24. It would seem that John Wilkes Booth and his family were somewhat tied by destiny to Abraham Lincoln and his family. Booth as you may recall was Lincoln's assassin. However, it should be noted that Booth had a brother who saved Lincoln's son a few years earlier on a train platform in New Jersey.

25. It is a bit of a sad reality, but Abraham Lincoln has no living, direct descendants.

26. John Wilkes Booth and Abraham Lincoln two crossed paths a number of times. In fact, Booth and Lincoln can be seen in the same photograph that was taken during the President's second inauguration.

27. When was Lincoln assassinated? It was actually on a Good Friday, which is why a lot of people have associated religious significance to his death.

28. When campaigning against Douglas, Lincoln actually won the popular vote. Ironically though, he lost during the actual elections.

29. It looks like Lincoln wasn't destined for a seat at the senate since he ran for a senatorial seat twice and lost both times.

30. He may not have been bound for the senate, but he did serve a term in the House of Representatives.

31. Lincoln didn't attend his father's funeral.

32. At his funeral Lincoln's coffin was actually opened a total of five times.

33. Okay so the people back then were really superstitious. On that note, when asked what Lincoln's shoe size was, people would usually say it is somewhere between size 12 and 14 – no one wanted to say size 13.

34. Abraham Lincoln was actually the very first President to sport a beard.

35. In 1876 grave robbers tried to steal Lincoln's body, but were foiled.

36. Honest Abe would have been long gone before he became President except for the fact that there were people who saved his life he was young. This actually happened twice.

37. The Lincoln family is one that was beset by tragedy – Abraham was estranged from his father, and his mother died by poisoned milk.

38. Abe Lincoln knew the strategic value of timely communication during war. Not only did he suspend the postal service to deter enemy communications, he used the telegraph like we use email today to communicate with his Generals. He wasn't squeamish about technology.

39. And of course, he was the very first American President to ever use the telegraph.

40. One of his favorite meals was chicken casserole, which he ate regularly at the White House.

41. But chicken casserole wasn't his number one favorite food – believe it or not his favorite was fruit.

42. His cat, Tabby, actually ate at the dinner table of the White House.

43. He also had a pet dog which he named Fido.

44. Abe Lincoln was actually the very first President who was born outside of the original 13 states of the US.

45. Do you love Thanksgiving? Well, it was Abe Lincoln who declared it as a national holiday.

46. Honest Abe was a very busy man before he got elected as President of the USA. Apart from being a lawyer, he also became a postmaster, and an owner of a general store.

47. Lincoln was actually the brains behind the creation of the US Secret Service. One of their early tasks was to stop the counterfeiting of US currency.

48. Lincoln was so popular that his corpse was valued at $200,000 – that was the ransom that the grave robbers wanted to ask until the men of the secret service caught them before they could execute their plans.

49. Abraham Lincoln actually tested the rifles that were to be issued to the US military. He tested the said firearms outside of the White House; which was illegal, by the way.

50. Abe Lincoln could have died earlier in 1864 when Confederate Troops attacked Washington. He owed his life to Colonel Oliver Wendell Holmes Jr. who yelled him down during the gunfire.

51. He had the biggest feet amongst all US presidents.

52. Abe Lincoln actually didn't sleep in his appointed White House bedroom. He slept in his office.

53. He was a man who would never give up. For instance, do you know that he lost in the elections 5 times at different electoral positions until he finally won the Presidency?

54. To date, there are more books written about Abraham Lincoln than any other US President.

55. Throughout his life he battled with depression (although they didn't call it that in his day). He fought against depression during times of victory, and he struggled hard against it when losses and failure came his way.

56. Abe Lincoln and Charles Darwin were actually born on the very same day.

57. Abraham Lincoln was actually a licensed bar tender.

58. Abe was six foot four inches tall, but his wife Mary was only five feet two inches.

59. Before Abe married Mary, he also had another girlfriend who was named Mary.

60. John Parker, Lincoln's bodyguard the day he was assassinated wasn't at his post. No one knows where he was at the time.

61. John Kennedy and Abraham Lincoln shared a lot of coincidences. For instance, both John F. Kennedy and Abraham Lincoln were shot in the head on a Friday.

62. Both successors to Lincoln and Kennedy were named Johnson.

63. John F. Kennedy was shot in a car – a Ford Lincoln. On the other hand, Abraham Lincoln was shot in the Ford Theater.

64. Both Abe and John's family names have 7 letters.

Chapter 10: Lincoln's Legacy

If you could survey the people in the Union back in 1863, you would find that Abraham Lincoln wasn't thought to be one of the greatest Presidents of the United States. However, fast forward a few centuries later and the opinion of the American people has changed.

A Change of Heart in the 20th Century

Back in 1982, political scientists and historians were surveyed on who they thought were the best American Presidents in history. The survey was conducted by the Chicago Tribune.

There were several factors that were to be considered when making their choice, which included the following:

- Character/integrity
- Appointments
- Political skills
- Crisis management
- Accomplishments
- Leadership qualities

The list that these well-informed men and scholars compiled included some of history's brightest. Figures like Harry Truman, Woodrow Wilson, Andrew Jackson, Thomas Jefferson, Theodore Roosevelt, George Washington, and of course Franklin Roosevelt were part of the final list.

However, none of these men were able to top Abraham Lincoln.

Roosevelt was number two after Lincoln, but when the man's character was the factor being considered, Lincoln won by a mile. This was the case when comparing Lincoln with all the others.

When asked if the general public would consider Abraham Lincoln as the best President in the history of the United States, these historians and political scientists believed that the general populace would agree with their assessment.

The Near Mythical Status

So, how did Abraham Lincoln turn the tide from a general public that had a rather poor evaluation of his performance to that of an adoring following? It was not happenstance really, but it was part of the brilliance of his character.

He chose the right people for the job. He was able to find really good Generals and other Officers during the Civil War, which eventually culminated in the surrender of General Lee, and thus the end of the war.

That boosted his public approval – but that wasn't all. A week later something would happen that would cement his name and fame in the annals of history – he would die a martyr.

His assassin thought that he would be doing a great service to the south by murdering the current President. Yes, he was successful in the act, but he failed in his intent. Several days after his death, the public began worshipping Lincoln.

There were even those who, maybe in a fit of religious frenzy, compared Abraham Lincoln to Jesus Christ. The media hailed him as the savior of the Union and the liberator of slaves.

Yes, things jumped to Biblical proportions during those days. A lot of people saw him as one who had given his life for the liberty of others.

Abraham Lincoln issued a lot of pardons during his Presidency, which people greatly respected. Yes, he declared martial law and held a tight grip of the country while everyone was at war, yet the pardons showed that he didn't do it for power or ambition.

The Activist President

Why would Abraham Lincoln become the activist President of his time? Well, he had to. The country entered into Civil War, and there were multiple factions even amongst those who called themselves allies. To overcome this and secure victory, Lincoln had to be bold and courageous in his approach.

Historians have always highly regarded Abraham Lincoln's status in America's popular culture. They accord him not only with what he accomplished, but also by how he was able to accomplish it.

Indeed, he put the Union first even above his own personal needs and troubles – and that demanded a lot of commitment. That is one thing that Lincoln was able to demonstrate time and again.

This was demonstrated in his personal life. His wife's family was deep in the practice of slavery – that was one of the tools they used to obtain their financial and social status. By ending slavery, he was valuing the African American's freedom above the desires of his wife's family.

To obtain his goals he also needed to have careful timing, patience, and of course shrewd calculations. It would require great sacrifice of himself to establish a more unified collection of states and a stronger Presidential leadership. He believed the country should unite not only under one banner, but also should march under the command of one office.

Decisive Leadership

Abraham Lincoln emancipated slaves and established and put to practice what was a principle that his predecessors had only imagined – equality for all.

Others strove to break that union and assail the freedom of other men. His life's work and legacy united the states and made people truly free – or at least according to a certain degree as mandated by law. Indeed, by the time of his death Abraham Lincoln left a United States that was truly free and truly whole.

On more than one occasion, Lincoln had to execute the powers of his office – something that others thought was against the decorum of the day. For instance, he called out state militias to expand the federal army.

He blockaded ports in the south, and he even closed the postal service so that they may not give aid to the states that seceded from the Union. In this effort he spent more than two million dollars in government funds – and he did that without congressional appropriation.

He made it a practice to suspend the writ of habeas corpus in times of war. He ordered the arrest of people who were suspected as traitors. And on New Year's Day of 1863 he issued the Emancipation Proclamation.

To do all of this, it required one who knew how to navigate the law and to expertly move forward with an iron grip.

Was there opposition? Of course, there was. He encountered opposition with pretty much every move he made. He clashed with members of Congress and he even clashed against the Supreme Court.

A Lasting Legacy

What was really his greatest achievement? Some would say that he transformed the White House into its modern version – one that is empowered with the full force of executive authority and the ability to enforce that power during times of great national crisis. During his Presidency, Abraham Lincoln clearly demonstrated that.

There is of course a duality to all that he achieved. Some would highlight his preservation of the Union, while others would emphasize his being the great emancipator.

If we are to understand his legacy, then we should take in everything that the man has ever contributed – solidarity for the nation and freedom and equal opportunity for all. You can't have a Lincoln that holds to one and let go of the other. And that maybe his legacy: to know that the power lies in you to act and to will and to do. To move boldly and decisively, breaking any barrier, be it political, social, or even racial, in order to do what is right acting "with malice towards none."

Conclusion

Thanks again for taking the time to read this book!

You should now have a good understanding of Abraham Lincoln, the incredible life he lived, and the impact he had on the United States of America.

If you enjoyed this book, please take the time to leave me a review on Amazon. I appreciate your honest feedback, and it really helps me to continue producing high quality books.